7.08

# FORENSIC EVIDENCE:
# HAIRS AND FIBERS

DARLENE STILLE

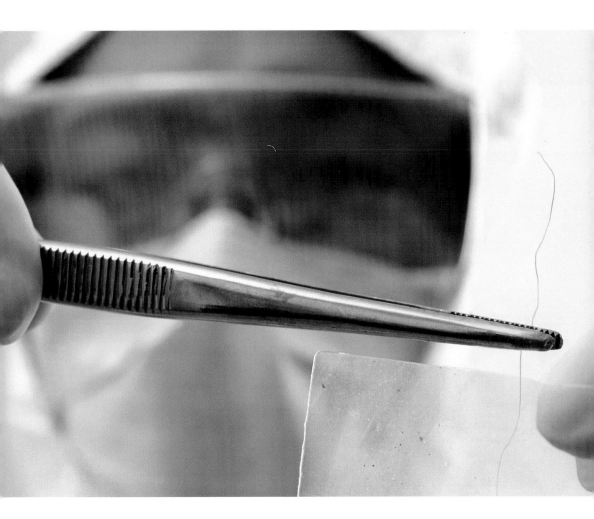

🌳 Crabtree Publishing Company

www.crabtreebooks.com

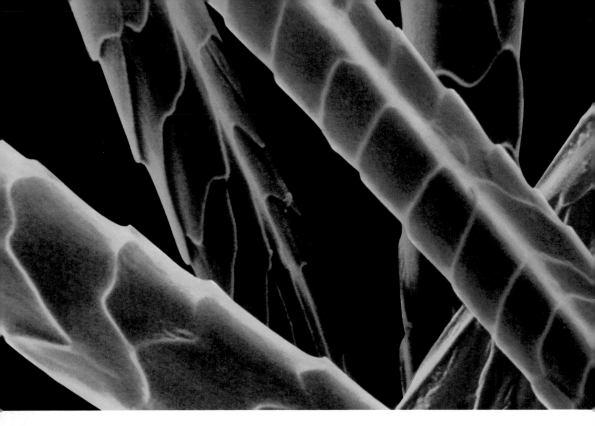

**Crabtree Publishing Company**
PMB 16A,
350 Fifth Avenue,
Suite 3308
New York, NY 10118

616 Welland Avenue,
St. Catharines, Ontario
L2M 5V6

Content development by
Shakespeare Squared

www.ShakespeareSquared.com

Published by Crabtree
Publishing Company © 2008

First published in Great Britain
in 2008 by ticktock Media Ltd,
2 Orchard Business Centre,
North Farm Road,
Tunbridge Wells, Kent, TN2 3XF

ticktock project editor:
  Ruth Owen
ticktock project designer:
  Sara Greasley
ticktock picture researcher:
  Lizzie Knowles

With thanks to: Series Editors Honor Head and Jean Coppendale
and Consultant John Cassella, Principal Lecturer in Forensic Science,
Department of Forensic Science, Staffordshire University, UK

Picture credits (t=top; b=bottom; c=centre; l=left; r=right):
age fotostock/ SuperStock: 12. brandXpictures: 29. Dr Tony Brain/
Science Photo Library: 15r. Andrew Brookes/ Corbis: OFC. Dr
Jeremy Burgess/ Science Photo Library: 31t. Scott Camazine/
Alamy: 14l. Michael Donne/ Science Photo Library: 26. Richard
Dunkley/ Getty Images: 25. Mauro Fermariello/ Science Photo
Library: 1, 7t, 11. Steve Gschmeissner/ Science Photo Library: 8bl, 9,
13t, 13b. Jupiter Images: 4c. Mikael Karlsson/ Alamy: 22. Medical-
on-line/ Alamy: 8br. Phototake Inc./ Alamy: 14-15c. Science Photo
Library: 2-3, 24t. Dr Jurgen Scriba/ Science Photo Library: 18.
Shutterstock: 4b, 5tl, 5tr, 8t x3, 10, 16, 17, 20-21, 23t, 24cl, 27b, 28
all. Andrew Syred/ Science Photo Library: 19, 23b. Tek Images/
Science Photo Library: 5b, 6-7b. Tim Wright/ Corbis: 27t.

Every effort has been made to trace copyright holders, and we
apologize in advance for any omissions. We would be pleased
to insert the appropriate acknowledgments in any subsequent
edition of this publication.

**Library and Archives Canada Cataloguing in Publication**

Stiller, Darlene
    Forensic evidence : hairs and fibers / Darlene Stiller.

(Crabtree contact)
Includes index.
ISBN 978-0-7787-3808-4 (bound).
--ISBN 978-0-7787-3830-5 (pbk.)

    1. Criminal investigation--Juvenile literature. 2. Hair--
Analysis--Juvenile literature. 3. Fibers--Analysis--Juvenile literature.
4. Forensic sciences--Juvenile literature. 5. Evidence, Criminal--
Juvenile literature. I. Title. II. Series.

HV8077.5.H34S75 2008        j363.25'62        C2008-901527-4

**Library of Congress Cataloging-in-Publication Data**

Stiller, Darlene.
    Forensic evidence : hairs and fibers / Darlene Stiller.
        p. cm. -- (Crabtree contact)
    Includes index.
    ISBN-13: 978-0-7787-3830-5 (pbk. : alk. paper)
    ISBN-10: 0-7787-3830-2 (pbk. : alk. paper)
    ISBN-13: 978-0-7787-3808-4 (reinforced library binding : alk. paper)
    ISBN-10: 0-7787-3808-6 (reinforced library binding : alk. paper)
    1. Criminal investigation. 2. Hair--Analysis. 3. Fibers--Analysis. 4.
Evidence, Criminal. 5. Forensic sciences. I. Title. II. Series.

    HV8077.5.H34.S75 2008
    363.25'62--dc22

                                        2008012854

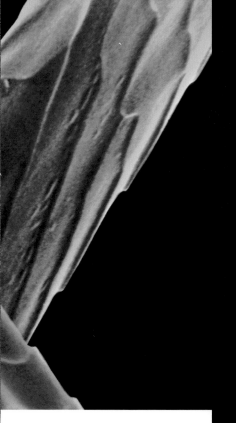

# Contents

# CHAPTER 1

# DIAMOND ROBBERY!

There has been a robbery at a jewelry store.

The robber stole diamond rings from the store's safe.

Safe

The diamond rings are worth almost **two million dollars**.

The robber cut the wires to the burglar alarm.
The robber smashed the store's **CCTV cameras**.

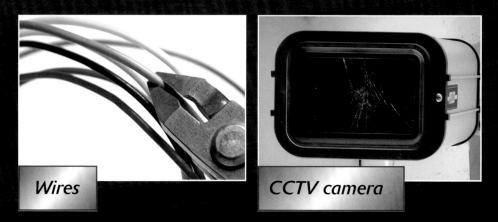

*Wires*

*CCTV camera*

No one saw the robbery happen.
At first, it seems there are no clues at the **crime scene**.

## Is it a perfect crime?

The police call for
the **Crime Scene
Investigators** (CSIs).

*Crime Scene
Investigator*

The CSIs know that criminals always leave clues. It may be
a hair, or a tiny piece of their clothing, called a **fiber**.

These little clues are called
**trace evidence**.

# CHAPTER 2

# LOOKING FOR TRACES

## Crime scene investigators search a crime scene for fingerprints, hairs, and fibers.

The CSIs wear gloves, masks, shoe covers, and white overalls.

The gloves prevent the CSIs from leaving their own fingerprints at the crime scene. The overalls prevent the CSIs from dropping their own hairs at the crime scene, or fibers from their own clothing.

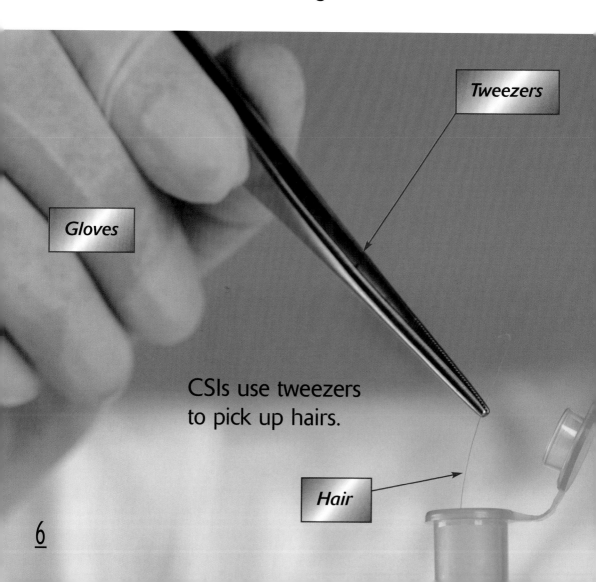

Tweezers

Gloves

CSIs use tweezers to pick up hairs.

Hair

CSIs use special vacuum cleaners to clean floors and surfaces at a crime scene.

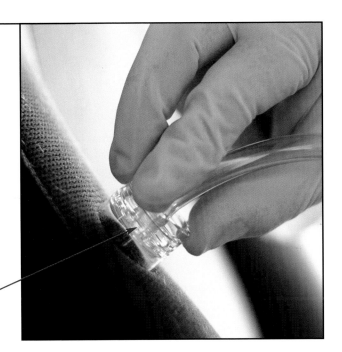

**Vacuum cleaner**

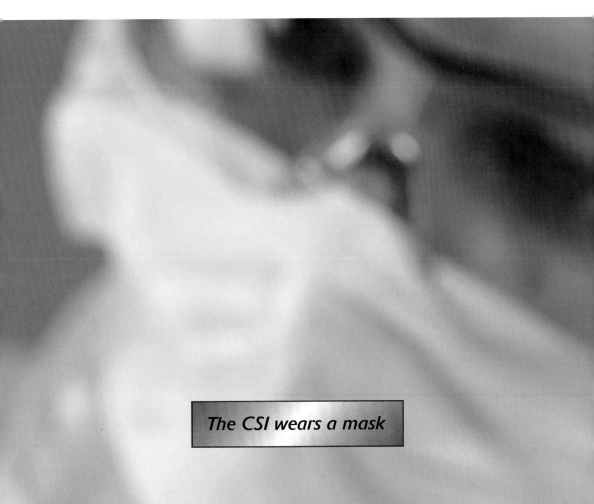

**The CSI wears a mask**

# Hair found at a crime scene can fall from any part of the criminal's body.

Different types of hair grow on the face, arms, and legs.

Old hairs fall out as new hairs grow.
About 100 hairs fall out of your head every day.

Hair can also come from a criminal's clothing,
from a pet, or from a fur coat.

All hairs look different under a microscope.

*Horse's hair*

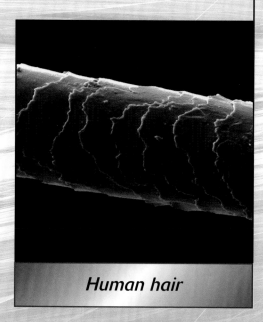

*Human hair*

# Sometimes hairs can get pulled out in a struggle or by accident.

A part of the hair, called the **follicle**, is in the skin. When a hair is pulled out, the follicle stretches.

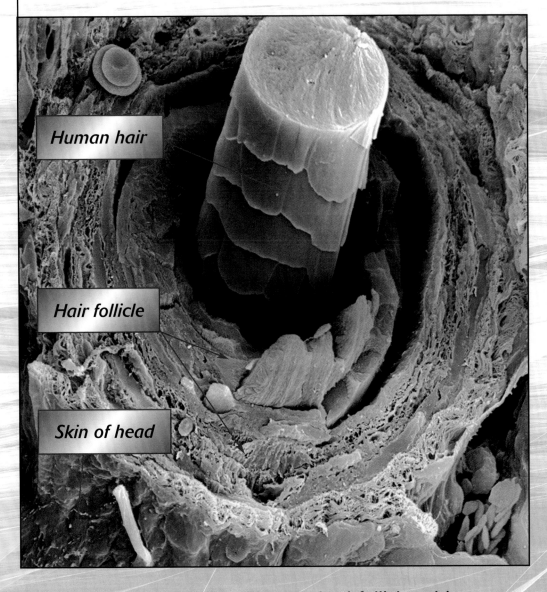

Human hair

Hair follicle

Skin of head

If CSIs find several hairs with stretched follicles, this could mean there was a struggle at the crime scene.

The CSIs find no fingerprints at the jewelry shop. The robber must have worn gloves.

They find no fibers.

But they do find some hairs, and one very interesting clue...

...a short, white hair.

---

The trace evidence is put in special plastic evidence bags.

CSIs at a crime scene must be very careful. One piece of evidence cannot touch another piece of evidence. Different pieces of evidence are put in separate bags. The evidence bag is labeled.

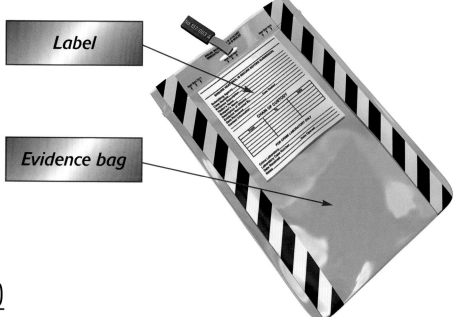

Label

Evidence bag

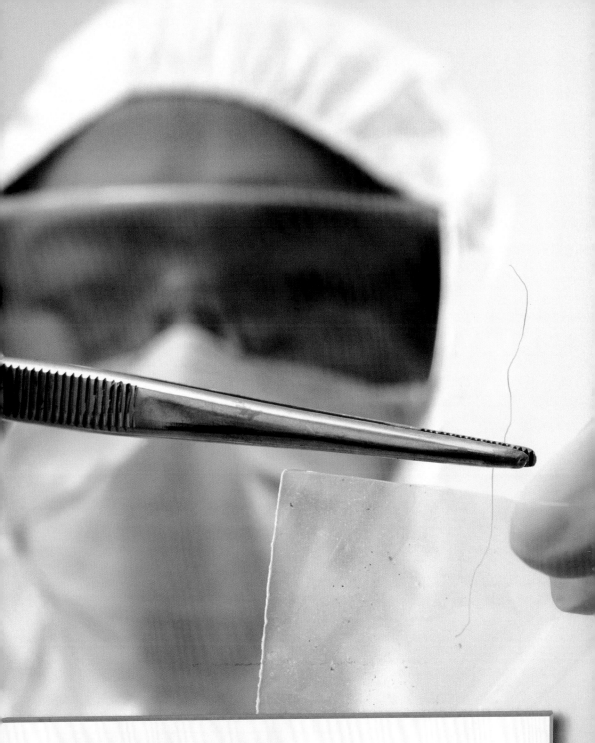

## NEED TO KNOW

If the police have a **suspect**, they can collect hairs from that person. The suspect's hair, and a hair from the crime scene might match.

# CHAPTER 3

# AT THE LAB

The evidence bags and the vacuum cleaner bags are taken to the **crime lab**.

A **forensic scientist** examines the hairs under a powerful microscope.

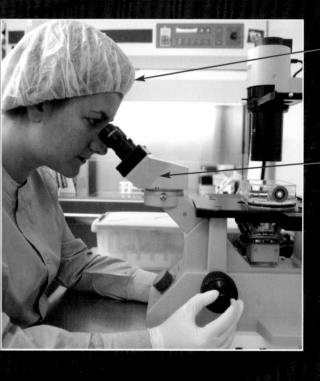

Forensic scientist

Microscope

First, she checks to find out if the hairs are from an animal or a human.

If a hair is human, the forensic scientist checks if it's rough, smooth, straight, or curly. This tells the scientist what part of the body the hair came from. It can also tell the scientist what **race** the person is.

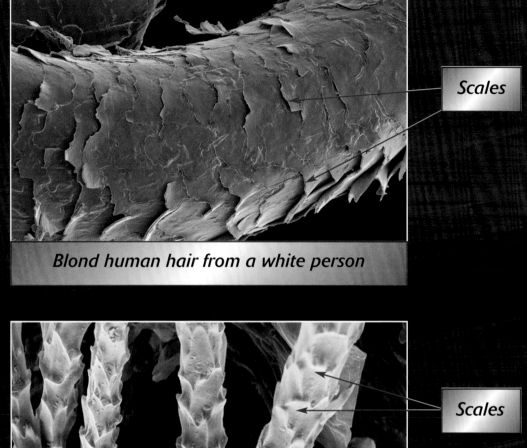

Scales

Blond human hair from a white person

Scales

Skin

Dog hairs

# NEED TO KNOW

Hairs are covered in scales. Scales overlap like shingles on a roof. Forensic scientists can use scale patterns to tell if a hair is from a human or an animal.

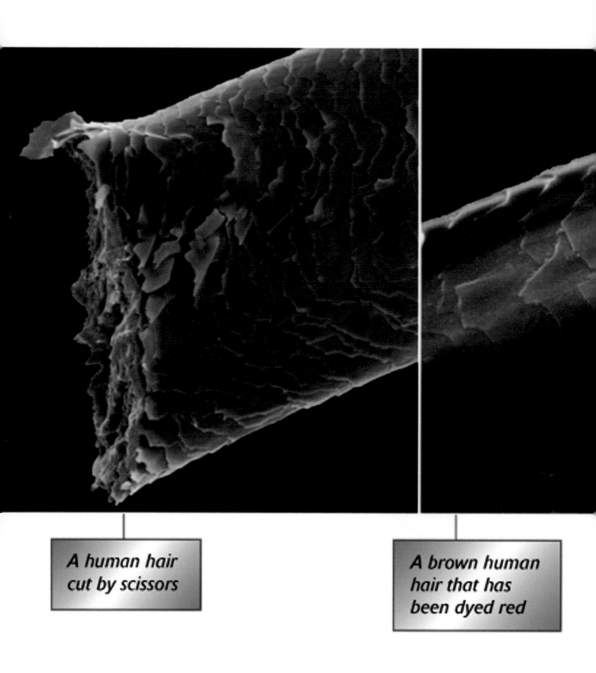

A human hair cut by scissors

A brown human hair that has been dyed red

Hairs can give forensic scientists clues to a **suspect's hairstyle**.

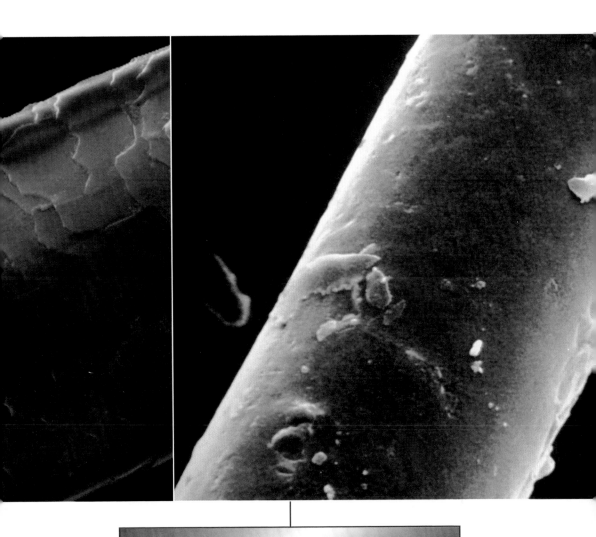

*A permed hair. The scales have been stripped away by the perm chemicals.*

Forensic scientists can tell if a hair was cut by scissors or a razor.

If CSIs find a human hair at a crime scene, the forensic scientists can do a **DNA** test.

Cells in our body and hair are **unique**.
Cells contain unique information called DNA.

Identical twins

Only identical twins have the same DNA.

A DNA test can be done on a single hair.

Special machines "read" the DNA.
They show the information in a pattern called a profile.

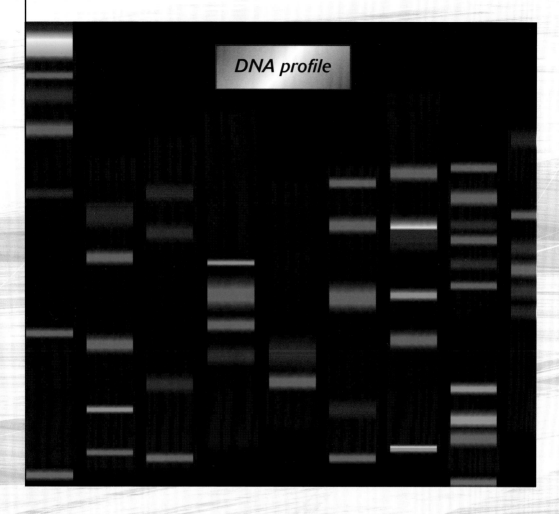

DNA profile

## Police databases store DNA profiles.

The profiles are from people who have been
arrested for a crime in the past.

Sometimes the police can match a DNA
profile from a hair at a crime scene to a
DNA profile on their database.

## This leads them to a suspect.

# Forensic scientists can test hair to find out if a person was taking drugs.

When a person uses drugs, chemicals from the drugs stay in a certain position in the person's hair. As the hair grows, it acts like a **timeline** showing when the person took drugs.

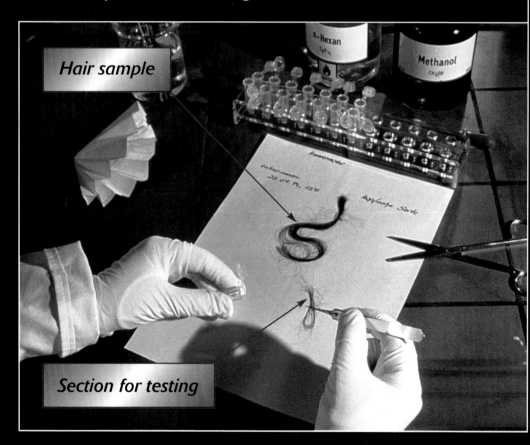

Hair sample

Section for testing

Hair grows at a steady rate. Forensic scientists can cut a hair sample into sections. Hair from close to the head will be only weeks old. Hair from further down the sample will be months old. The hair sections can be matched to time periods and tested for drugs.

Cat hair

Most of the hairs found at the jewelry shop belong to the shop's workers.

The short, white hair does not belong to any of the workers.

# It is not a human hair!

## RESULT
The white hair is from a white cat. No one at the shop owns a cat. Did the hair come from the robber's cat?

# CHAPTER 4

# A COLD CASE HEATS UP!

The police are confused.
But then there is a breakthrough!

# There is a robbery at another jewelry shop.

A **witness** sees a car speeding from the crime scene. The witness writes down the car's license plate number.

# The CSIs search the new crime scene.

They find more white hairs.
They also find fibers on a door handle.

Did the robber catch his or her clothes
on the door handle?

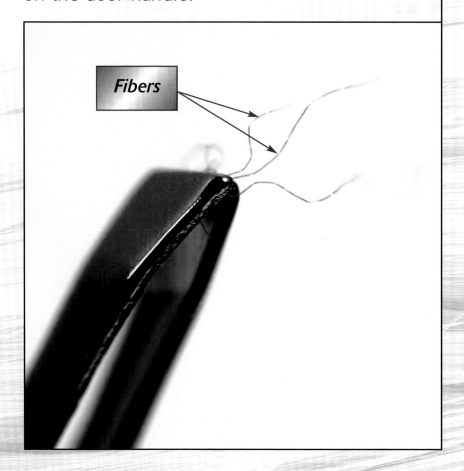

Fibers

Fibers at a crime scene can come from clothes,
towels or sheets, and carpets or curtains.

Fibers from a carpet can stick to hair on a body.
Fibers from clothes can stick to a chair.

# Back at the lab, the forensic scientists want to know if the fibers are natural or human-made.

Natural fibers come from plants or animals.

Wool fibers come from sheep and other animals with wooly coats.

Cotton fibers come from cotton plants.

*Cotton plant*

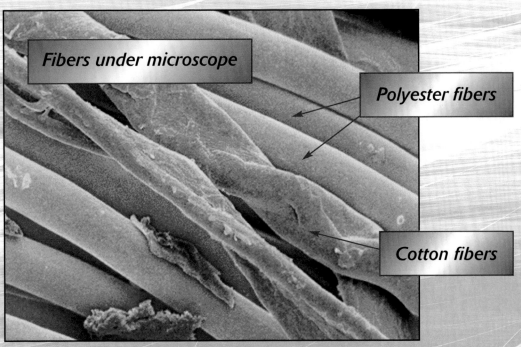

*Fibers under microscope*

*Polyester fibers*

*Cotton fibers*

Human-made fibers such as nylon, rayon, and polyester are made from chemicals.

The forensic scientists examine the fibers from the jewelry store under a microscope.

*Angora wool fibers*

*Angora goat*

## RESULT

The fibers are natural.
They are blue angora wool.

# The wool fibers are dyed dark blue.

Dyes can be made from plants, but most modern dyes are made from chemicals.

*Wool being dyed dark blue*

Every batch of dye is a little bit different. **Manufacturers** label and keep records of each batch of dye that they make.

25

# BUILDING A CASE

The police track the car license plate from the second robbery. They visit the car's owner.

The police search the car owner's house. They find a blue angora wool sweater.

---

But they find no signs of a **white cat**.

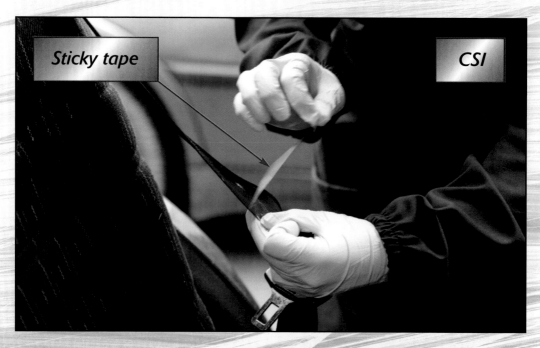

*Sticky tape*

*CSI*

CSIs search the car. They find more fibers!

**RESULT**
The fibers match the carpet at the second jewelry store. The car owner is now a suspect.

# The police track down the factory that made the dye and the sweater.

The factory owner tells the police that she used the dye to make just 100 blue angora sweaters.

# The police go visit the suspect again.

A white cat jumps the fence from next door. It goes into the suspect's house.

**RESULT**
The neighbor's cat is a match for the white hair found at the crime scene.

# THE TRIAL

The police charge the suspect with the robbery.

In court, he says he is **innocent**!

## THE PROSECUTION

- The suspect's car was seen at the crime scene.

- Carpet fibers from the jewelry store were found in the car.

- The suspect owns a rare blue angora sweater.

• The suspect's neighbor owns a white cat.

## THE DEFENSE

- The suspect says he picked up the carpet fibers when he shopped at the jewelry store.

- He says his car was in a parking lot on the night of the robbery. The real robber took his car then put it back.

- The DEFENSE **lawyer** says the hair and fiber evidence is not strong enough to **convict** the suspect.

Jury

Suppose you are on the **jury**.
What would you vote:

# GUILTY OR NOT GUILTY?

# NEED-TO-KNOW WORDS

**CCTV camera** Closed-Circuit Television Camera. A camera that records what is happening and sends it to a TV screen where it can be watched or recorded.

**crime lab** A laboratory with equipment that is used for scientific experiments and tests on crime-scene evidence

**crime scene** Any place where a crime has happened

**Crime scene investigators (CSIs)** People who examine crime scenes and collect evidence

**DEFENSE** The lawyer or group of lawyers who try to prove in court that the person accused of the crime (the defendant) is innocent

**DNA** The special code in the center (or nucleus) of each person's cells. Our DNA makes us all unique.

**evidence** Facts and signs that can show what happened during a crime

**fiber** A tiny thread

**follicle** An opening on the surface of the skin through which hair grows

**forensic scientist** An expert who gathers detailed information from a crime scene and analyzes it to figure out what happened

**guilty** Having done wrong, such as committing a crime

**innocent** Free from guilt or blame

**jury** A group of people in a court who listen to all the evidence. Then they decide if the accused is innocent or guilty.

**lawyer** An expert in the law who is hired to speak in court and give people advice about the law

**manufacturers** Companies that make products

**race** A group of people with the same skin color or culture or ancestors

**suspect** A person who is thought to have committed a crime

**trace** A very small mark, sign, or substance that is left behind

**unique** The only one of its kind

**witness** Someone who saw a crime being committed or who has information about a crime

# NEED-TO-KNOW FACTS

- **Inside a hair**
  A hair is made up of three layers. The outer layer is called the cuticle. The cuticle is made of colorless scales that overlap each other. The cortex is the inner part of the hair. The cortex is important to forensic scientists because it has pigment. This is the material that gives hair its color. Inside the cortex is a tube called the medulla.

- **Haircut evidence**
  Forensic scientists can sometimes work out when someone last had a haircut. A newly-cut hair is square cut. After about three weeks, the hair tip begins to look rounded.

- **Time to shampoo**
  A forensic scientist can tell if you've washed your hair or not. The black spots on the hairs below are four-day-old dirt!

# CRIME ONLINE

*http://www.fbi.gov/page2/july07/trace070207.htm*
This site explains how the FBI used hair and fiber evidence to solve a crime.

*http://www.fbi.gov/kids/6th12th/6th12th.htm*
This site has information about how the FBI investigates crimes.

*http://www.howstuffworks.com/csi5.htm*
This site explores the world of CSI.

*www.sciencenewsforkids.org/articles/20041215/wordfind.asp*
This science site includes a crime lab wordsearch.

# INDEX

Printed in the U.S.A.